FIRMAMENT

STELLAR STITCHES FOR YOUR NEXT ADVENTURE

HUNTER HAMMERSEN

PANTSVILLE PRESS

Charts created with Stitchmastery Knitting Chart Editor.

ISBN: 978-0-9849982-9-6

First Printing, 2018

Printed in China

Pantsville Press

Maine

www.pantsvillepress.com

Contents

Introduction

This was supposed to be a hat pattern. Just one, single, simple, stand-alone hat pattern. Nothing fancy. I've done this many times before.

But then, when the hat was done, I found I couldn't stop playing with the stitch I'd used. Or rather, I couldn't stop playing with the technique that stitch used.

It isn't hard. All you do is pull an extra loop of yarn through the fabric you've already created and then work with that stitch a bit. And it isn't new. Very little in knitting is new, and I'm absolutely sure folks have been doing this for a long time. But it *is* unreasonably entertaining.

I called them dip stitches (because you dip your needle down into your fabric to create the extra stitches), and I couldn't get enough of them.

I figured I'd whip out another project and the obsession would fade. But no. That project didn't help at all. Nor did the one after that. Or the one after that. If anything, I found myself more entranced.

So I did the only thing I could think of. I asked you folks if you were as taken with these stitches as I was. It turned out you were.

I brought the patterns together into a little book. Then I added a primer on the technique, tucked in a mini stitch dictionary with variations on each of the stitches used in the patterns, shared all my feelings about hats and charts, and even worked in a little discussion on turning hat patterns into cowl patterns.

And now? Now I'm handing it over to you. Make the hats just as they're written (and enjoy all the compliments you'll get when you wear them). If you want to keep going (and I suspect you will), make a matching cowl. If you're still not ready to quit, play with one of the stitch variations included at the end. Or take the technique and come up with something all your own.

Whatever you make is sure to be lovely, and I suspect you'll be as enchanted as I am!

Hats

Gauge and Sizing: All the hats in this book are written in *lots* of sizes and gauges. That means you can use all sorts of yarn (fingering, sport, DK, and light worsted-weight yarns all work well). But you will need to check the chart at the start of each pattern to see which size works best for your head and your gauge.

Start by measuring your head (wrap a tape measure snugly around your head just above your eyebrows), then look at the chart. Let's say your head is 22.5 inches around, and the sizing chart for your pattern looks like this:

	5.5 SPI	6 SPI	6.5 SPI	7 SPI
108 STS	21.5	19.75	18.25	17
114 STS	22.75	21	19.25	18
120 STS	24	22	20.25	18.75
126 STS	25.25	23	21.25	19.75
132 STS	26.5	24.25	22.25	20.75
138 STS	27.5	25.25	23.25	21.75

The column on the left lists the pattern sizes (in stitches, abbreviated **sts**). The top row lists the gauges (in stitches per inch, abbreviated **spi**). The intersection of a column and row gives the head size (in inches) that a hat knit in that size and gauge will fit (remember hats have a bit of negative ease, and that's built into the measurements in the table).

If you have a 22.5-inch head, you'd scan through the numbers in the middle of the chart looking for 22.5 or things close to it (knitting is stretchy so 22, 22.25, 22.75 and 23 will all fit). I've highlighted the sizes that would work for a 22.5-inch head as an example. So you could make the 114-stitch size at 5.5 spi, the 120-stitch size at 6 spi, the 126-stitch size at 6 spi, or the 132-stitch size at 6.5 spi.

Pick whichever gauge gives you a fabric you like with your yarn.

Needles: Because the patterns are all written for so many gauges, I really can't tell you what needle size you'll want to use. The only way to figure that out is to swatch. That's always good advice (much better than using a specific needle size), but it's especially important for patterns in multiple gauges because you are very unlikely to use the same needle size to get 5.5 stitches per inch and 7 stitches per inch.

Swatch: Swatch the pattern shown in the Rib Chart for your hat (that's what determines fit). Always be sure you're measuring your gauge over a blocked swatch! Also, if you get a different gauge when you knit flat versus when you knit in the round, be sure you're swatching in the round for these projects.

Brim: You can easily adjust the height of your brim to suit your preferences. I like a fairly deep folded brim, so all the hats shown have the Rib Chart worked for 4-6 inches (then folded in half). But if you like a shallower folded brim or a straight brim, you can do that instead. I'd suggest working the Rib Chart for 1-2 inches if you're not going to fold it.

Remember that a hat will stretch a bit when it's on your head, so 5 inches of ribbing on your needles will be more like 2.25 inches of ribbing when you fold it in half and wear it. It's a good idea to either try the hat on and check that you like the depth or knit a few extra rounds to account for the height lost to stretching.

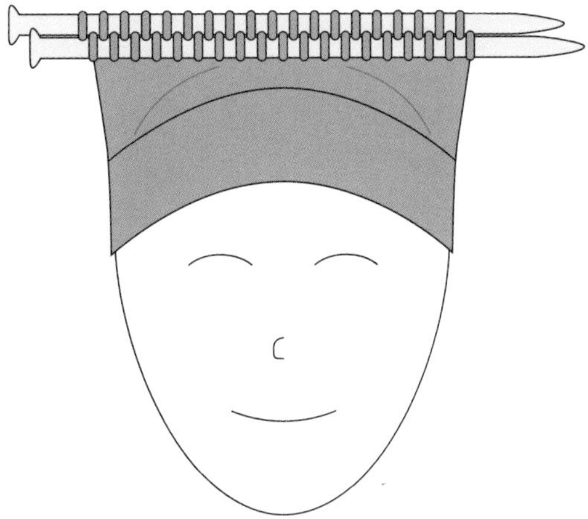

HAT HEIGHT: The decreases on these hats happen quickly (so fast that they actually gather up a bit of the hat fabric), and it can be tricky to judge how tall to make a hat with decreases like that.

I like to divide all my stitches on two long needles, hold them together, and try the hat on. It looks silly, but holding the stitches like that approximates how much of the height of the hat gets taken up by the fast decreases. If it's tall enough with the stitches held that way, it will be tall enough once you've worked the decreases.

FINISHING: Break the yarn leaving an 12-inch tail, thread the tail onto a darning needle, run it through the stitches at the top of the hat, and cinch it closed (I think it looks best if you loop through all of those stitches two or three times instead of once). Weave in your ends (be extra tidy if you want the hat to be reversible).

BLOCKING: Knitting looks better if it's blocked, and it's so easy to do that it really is worth the time.

Soak your knitting in cool water for 15 minutes (squeeze it when you put it in to make sure it's really soaked). Take it out and gently squeeze out the water (wrap it in a towel to press out even more if you're in a hurry). Shape your knitting (fold up the brim if you've made a folded brim) and let it dry.

You can either let it dry flat, or better yet, put it over something head shaped (mixing bowls, balloons, and wig stands all work well). That's really all there is to it!

Charts

I love charts. They're a great way to present a lot of information in a small space. But as much as I love them, I realize that they can seem a bit daunting if you're not used to them. Once you get to know them though, they're easy. The most important thing to remember is that charts show you a stylized picture of the right side of your work. Keep that in mind, and you're halfway there!

The easiest way to get to know a chart is to work through an example. So let's talk through this sample chart step by step. You can actually walk through this with scrap yarn if you want.

Say you've cast on 32 stitches, placed a start of round marker, and joined to work in the round. The next step is to work this chart.

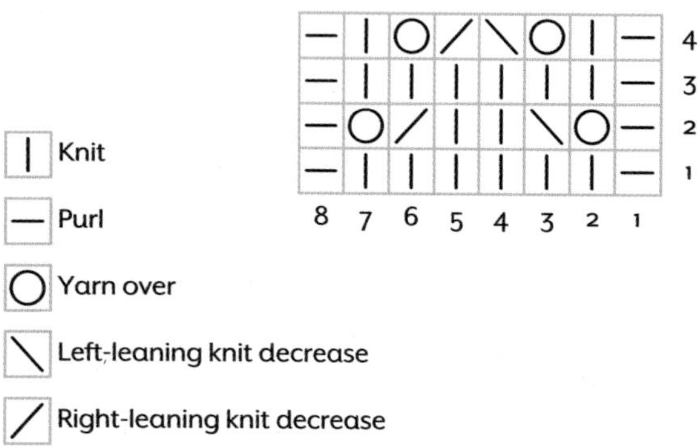

Take a look at the chart and notice that the rows are numbered 1-4 and the columns are numbered 1-8.

You'll always start with row 1 (on the bottom) and work your way up. And, because you're working in the round, you'll always start with the column 1 (on the right) and work your way left.

Each symbol represents a type of stitch (like knit or purl). There's a key to tell you what each symbol means.

Now all you have to do is start knitting. Just start at row 1, column 1, and read across the first row of the chart, one stitch at a time, making the stitches in the order they're shown.

I'll talk you through the example.

Row 1: purl 1, knit 6, purl 1.

Repeat those 8 stitches across the whole first round of your knitting. Once you get back to your start of round marker, move on to row 2.

Remember, all the charts in this book are for working in the round, so you're always working a right side row. So row 2 behaves just the same way (read the chart from right to left).

Row 2: purl 1, yarn over, left-leaning knit decrease, knit 2, right-leaning knit decrease, yarn over, purl 1.

Repeat those 8 stitches across the whole

second round of your knitting. When you get to your start of round marker, move on to row 3.

Row 3: purl 1, knit 6, purl 1.

Repeat those 8 stitches across the whole third round of your knitting. When you get to your start of round marker, move on to row 4.

Row 4: purl 1, knit 1, yarn over, left-leaning knit decrease, right-leaning knit decrease, yarn over, knit 1, purl 1.

Repeat those 8 stitches across the whole fourth round of your knitting. When you get to your start of round marker, go back to row 1 and start all over again.

Remember you're always repeating the stitches in each row of the chart all the way across a round (so here you work stitches 1-8 as many times as needed until you finish the whole round). And remember that you work through the chart from bottom to top and then start over again at the bottom (so here you work rows 1-4, then start over with row 1 and do it again).

That's really all there is to it. Just take it one stitch at a time, one row at a time, read the chart from right to left and from bottom to top, and you'll do great.

There's only one more thing to keep in mind. Sometimes you'll see a chart that looks a little funny because it has some missing spaces. It might look something like this.

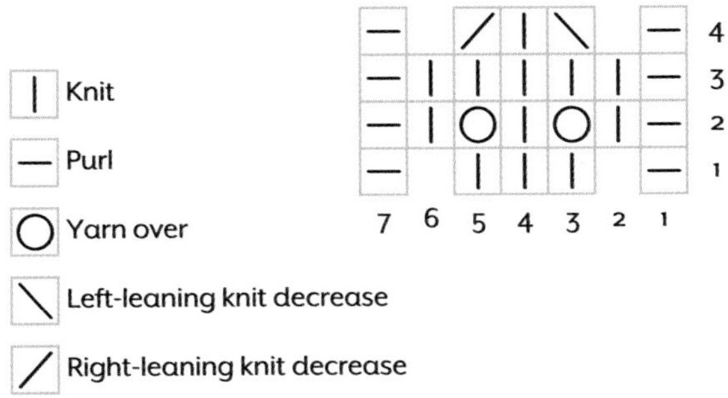

That happens when there are a different numbers of stitches on different rows (or when your fabric is getting narrower like at the top of a hat). See how the chart has you increase 2 stitches on row 2 and then decrease them away on row 4? Having the blank spots on rows that have fewer stitches keeps things as lined up as possible. So in this example it keeps the purl columns lined up, even though the stuff in between them is changing shape.

Don't worry about the missing spaces. You can just ignore them (yes, really!). You don't do anything with your yarn or needles when you see them, they're only a placeholder on the chart. Just let your eyes skip right over the blank spots, move on to the next stitch that has a symbol, and do whatever that symbol tells you to do.

Dip Stitches

To make a dip stitch, all you do is pick a spot on your fabric and pull a new loop of yarn through the fabric at that spot. That's really all there is to it!

There are two parts to the process (picking the spot and pulling the yarn through), and we'll talk a little about both.

The instructions for a particular dip stitch will always tell you to count left or right a certain number of stitches and down a certain number of rows. Let's look at an example.

Say the instructions told you to count left 2 stitches and down 5 rows. You'd find the second stitch on your left needle (that's counting left 2 stitches). Then, starting with the row of stitches below your needle, move down 5 rows (that's counting down 5 rows). The arrow on figure 1 shows you which stitch we're talking about.

The arrow on figure 2 shows you which stitch you'd go into if the instructions told you to count left 4 stitches and down 3 rows.

The arrow on figure 3 shows you which stitch you'd go into if the instructions told you to count right 2 stitches and down 4 rows.

Once you've found your target stitch, put the tip of your right needle between the legs of the

FIGURE 1
Left 2
Down 5

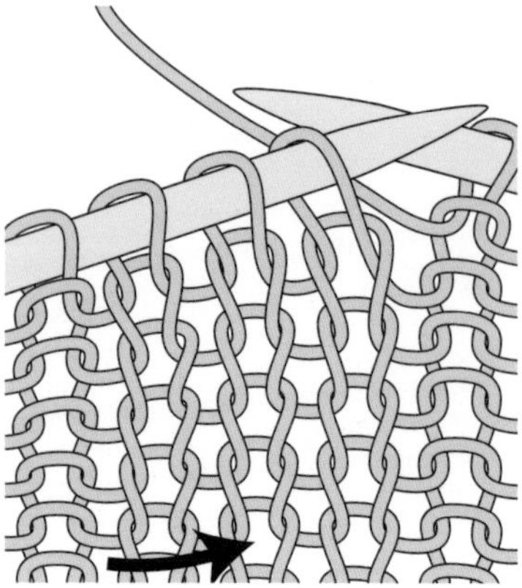

FIGURE 2
Left 4
Down 3

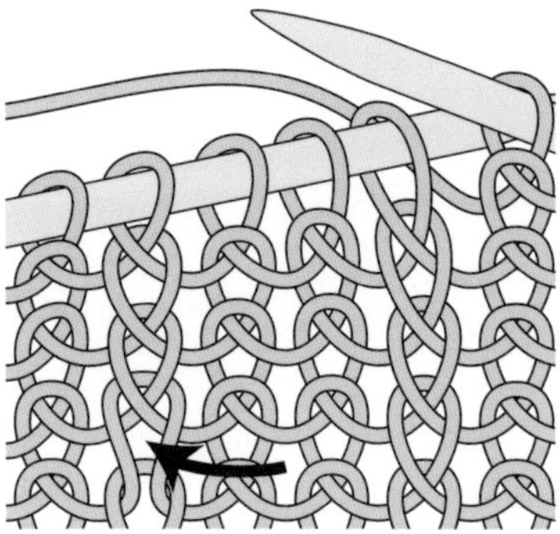

FIGURE 3
Right 2
Down 4

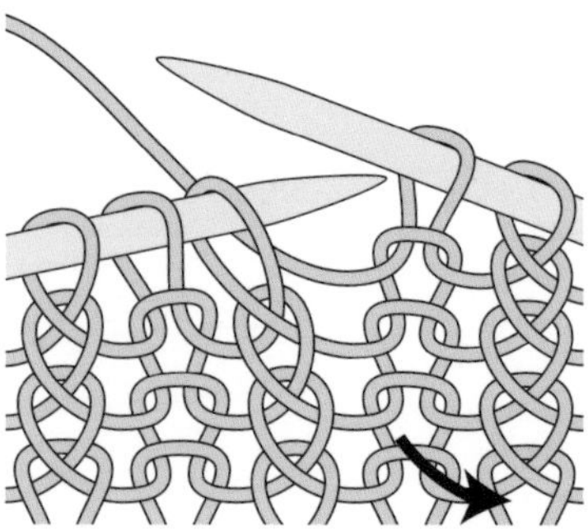

stitch, wrap your yarn around it (exactly the way you do to make a knit stitch), and pull the yarn back through the fabric.

You'll end up with a long loop of yarn on your right needle (figures 4, 5, and 6 show the results of the stitches in figures 1, 2, and 3). Treat this just like any other stitch. The charts for each pattern will tell you what to do with it for that particular pattern, but the idea is that it's now just another one of your stitches.

The illustrations on the following pages show you exactly how to do the stitches used in the patterns. There are also variations on each of the pattern stitches at the end of the book to get you started with your explorations. But you should feel free to experiment and find something you love!

Try changing your background fabric (ribbing, stockinette, or reverse stockinette all give very different looks). Try changing how far over and down you count to alter the length and angle of your new stitches. And remember, anything you can do with a regular stitch, you can do with your new stitches. Try using them on the front of a cable or as part of a lace motif. The variations are pretty much endless.

Oh, and do yourself a favor and take a look at the back side of your fabric from time to time. The long loops that make such a pretty pattern on the front often do great things on the back of the fabric, too.

FIGURE 4

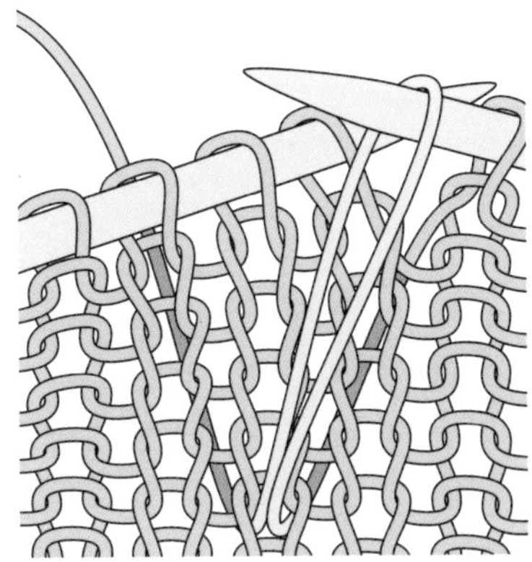

FIGURE 5

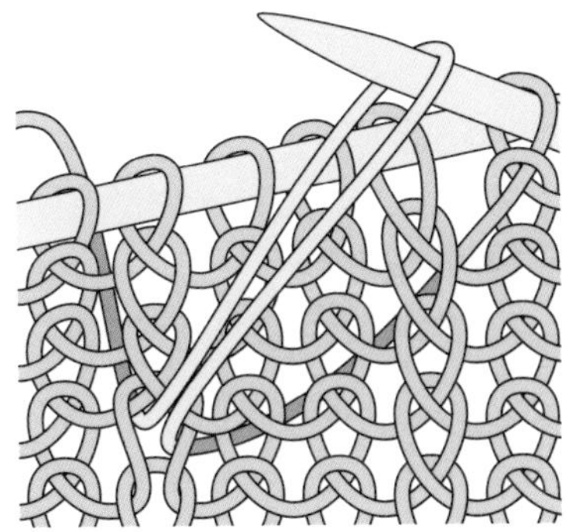

FIGURE 6

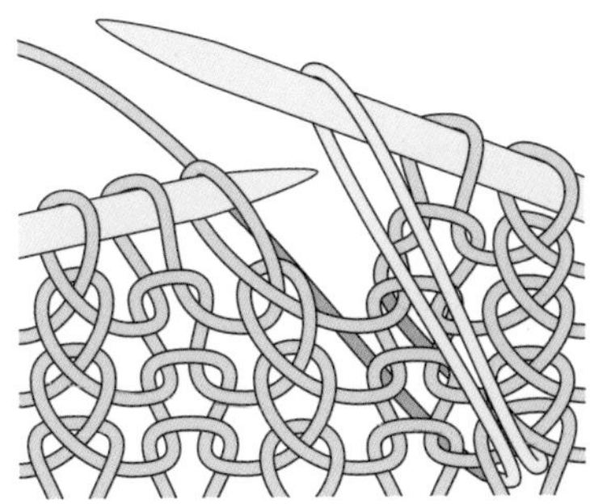

Constellate Dip Stitches

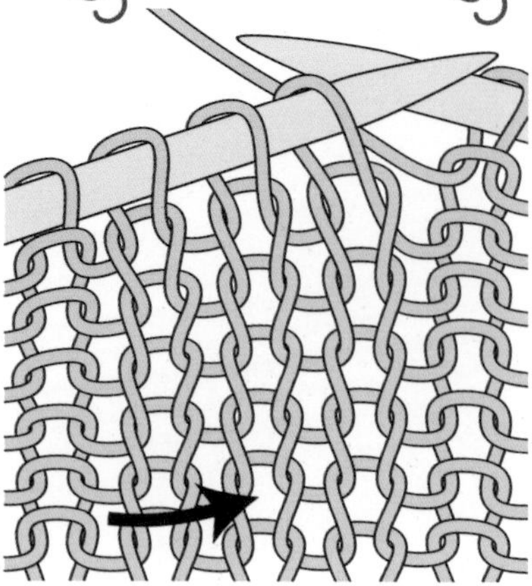

1: Dip Left—with yarn in back, count left 2 stitches and down 5 rows.

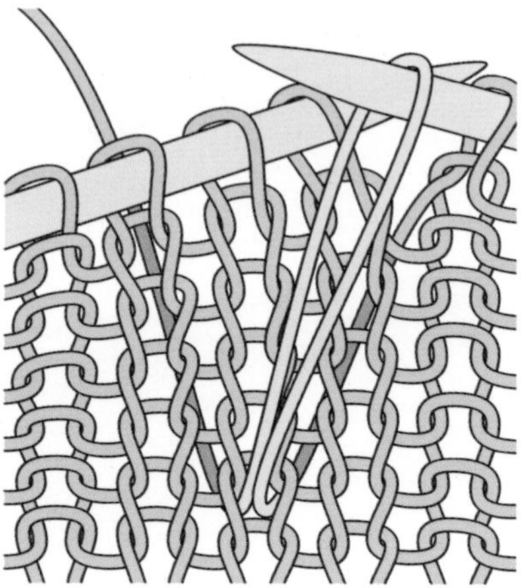

2: Put your right needle tip through the legs of that stitch, pull a loop of yarn through.

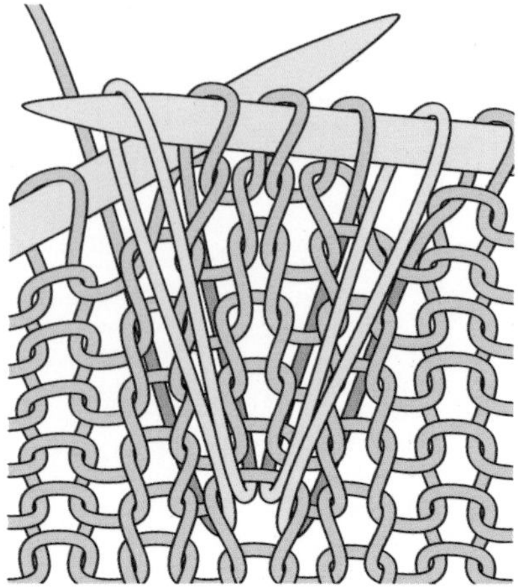

3: Dip Right—with yarn in back, count right 2 stitches and down 6 rows. Put your right needle tip through the legs of that stitch (it's the same one you went into before), pull a loop of yarn through.

Sidereal Dip Stitches

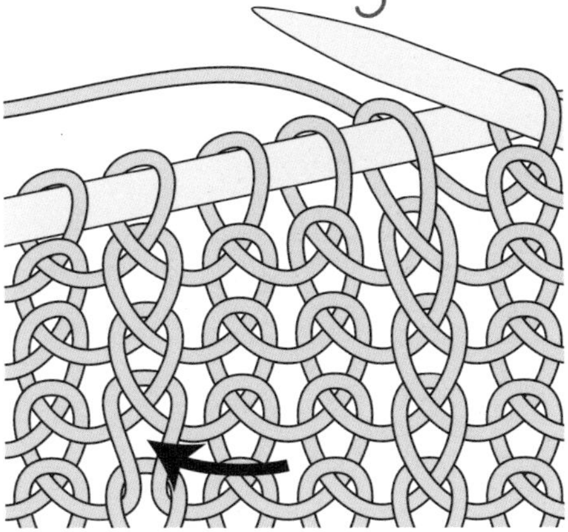

1: Dip Left—with yarn in back, count left 4 stitches and down 3 rows.

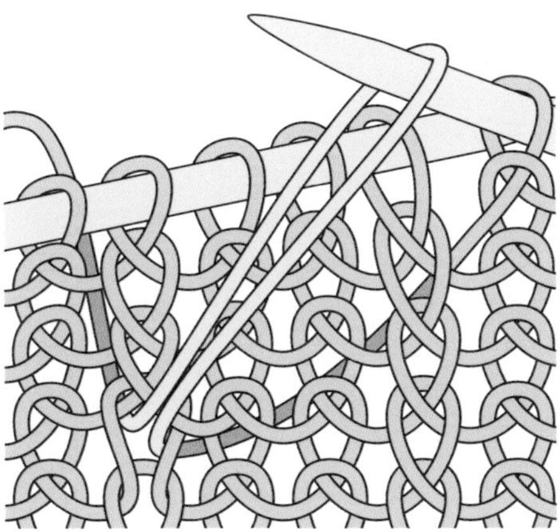

2: Put your right needle tip through the legs of that stitch, pull a loop of yarn through.

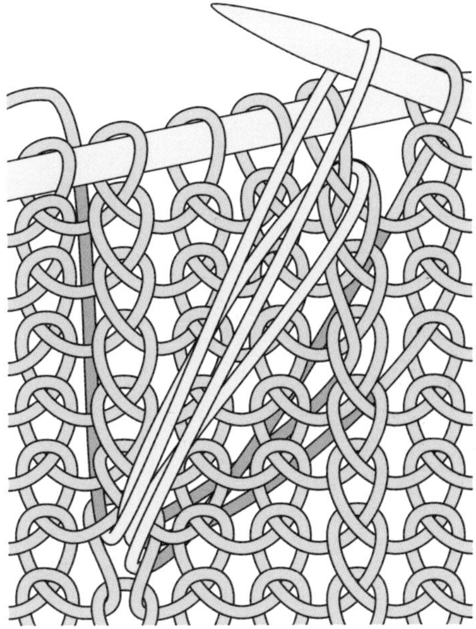

3: Dip Left—with yarn in back, count left 4 stitches and down 6 rows. Put your right needle tip through the legs of that stitch (it's the same one you went into before), pull a loop of yarn through.

Ecliptic Dip Stitches

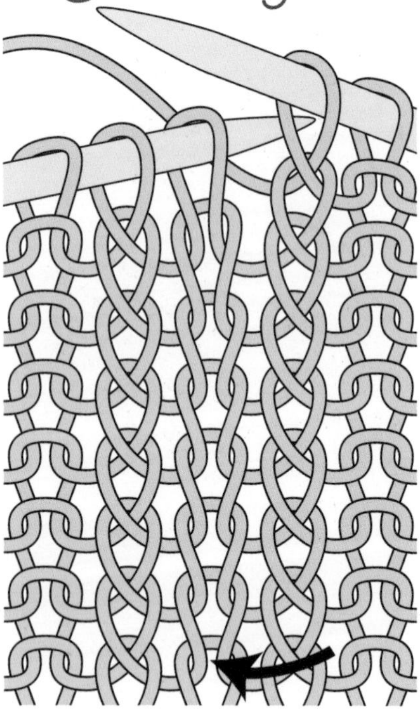

1: Dip Down—with yarn in back, count left 1 stitch and down 7 rows.

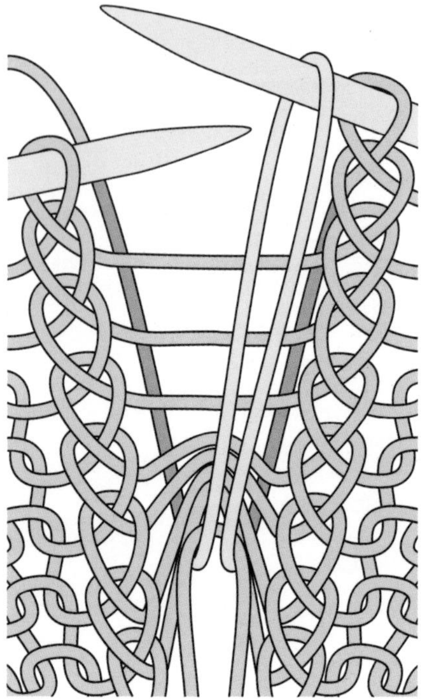

2: Put your right needle tip through the legs of that stitch, pull a loop of yarn through. Drop the first stitch off your left needle and let it run down until it's caught by your loop of yarn. You may need to tug on the fabric or yarn a bit to encourage the stitch to run all the way down.

Ephemeris Dip Stitches

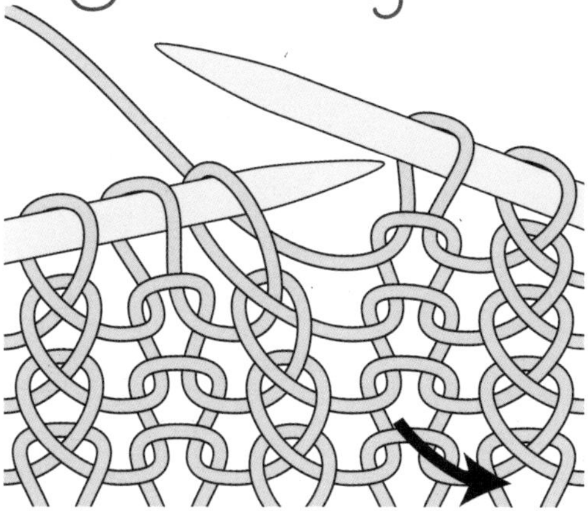

1: Dip Right—with yarn in back, count right 2 stitches and down 4 rows.

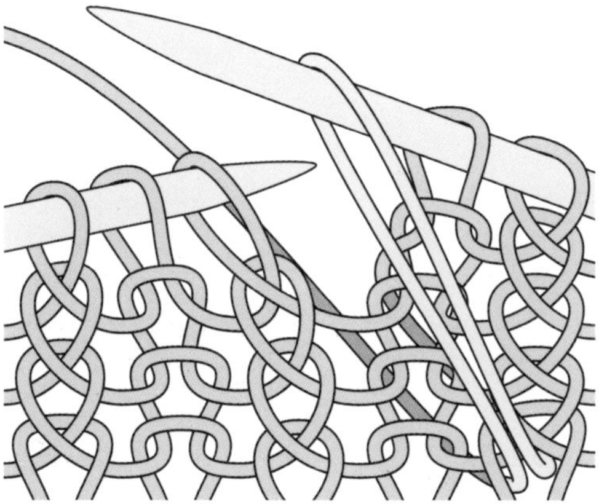

2: Put your right needle tip through the legs of that stitch, pull a loop of yarn through.

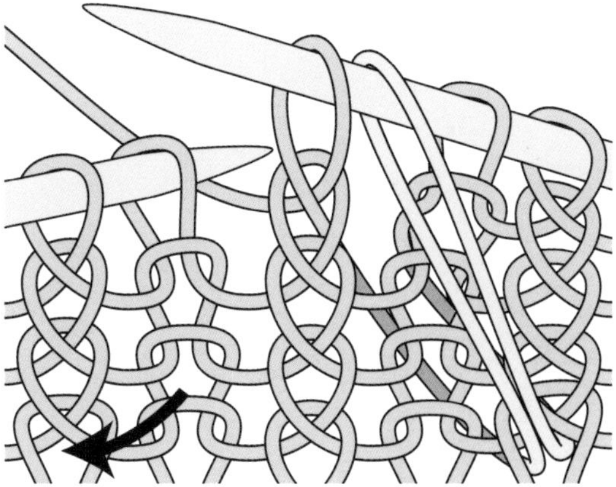

3: Dip Left—with yarn in back, count left 2 stitches and down 3 rows.

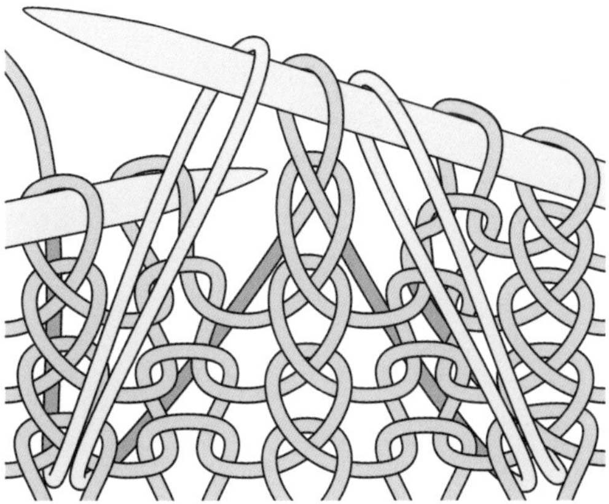

4: Put your right needle tip through the legs of that stitch, pull a loop of yarn through.

Constellate

Yarn: Made with 325 yards of Tosh Merino Light, a fingering-weight yarn by Madelinetosh, in the color Calligraphy. You may need up to 400 yards if you make a larger size or use a thinner yarn.

Size: Made in the 120-stitch size at a gauge of 6.5 stitches per inch. Use the chart to pick your gauge and size.

Notes: See the beginning of the book for more on how to pick a size, read a chart, make dip stitches, and decide how tall to make your hat.

	5.5 SPI	6 SPI	6.5 SPI	7 SPI
104 STS	20.75	19	17.5	16.25
112 STS	22.5	20.5	19	17.5
120 STS	24	22	20.25	18.75
128 STS	25.5	23.5	21.75	20
136 STS	27.25	25	23	21.25

3.25 needle
400 mts.

Cast on: Cast on 104 [112, 120, 128, 136] stitches. Place marker. Join for working in the round.

Brim: Work the Rib Chart until brim reaches desired height. Shown here at 4 inches.

Body: Work the Main Chart until hat reaches desired height before decreases. Stop after completing row 6 of the Main Chart. Shown here at 7 inches.

Decreases: Work the Decrease Chart once. 13 [14, 15, 16, 17] stitches remain.

Finishing: Remove marker, draw the yarn through remaining stitches. Weave in ends. Block.

Rib Chart

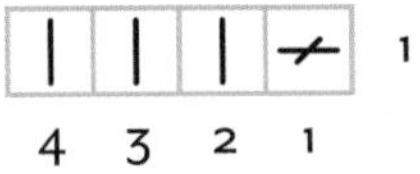

Main Chart

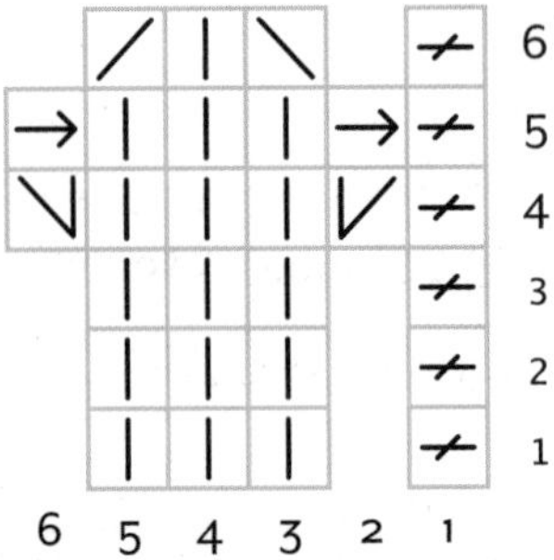

Decrease Chart

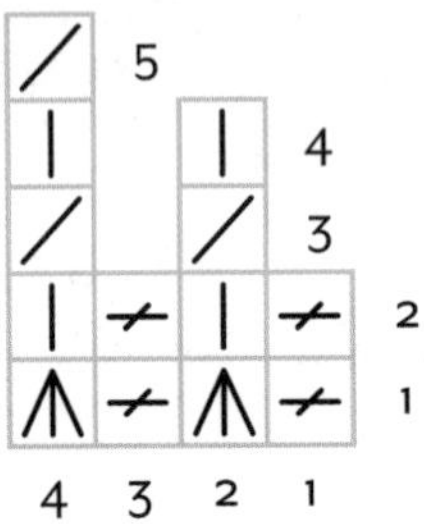

Dip Left: Yarn behind, count left 2 stitches and down 5 rows. Pull a loop through.

Dip Right: Yarn behind, count right 2 stitches and down 6 rows. Pull a loop through.

Left-leaning knit decrease: Slip 1 knitwise. Slip another 1 knitwise. Return slipped stitches to the left needle. Insert the right needle from the right to the left into the back loops of both stitches. Knit both together.

Right-leaning knit decrease: Knit 2 together.

Centered double knit decrease: Slip 2 together at the same time as if to knit 2 together. Knit 1. Pass the slipped stitches over.

Slip: Slip 1 as if to purl with yarn in back.

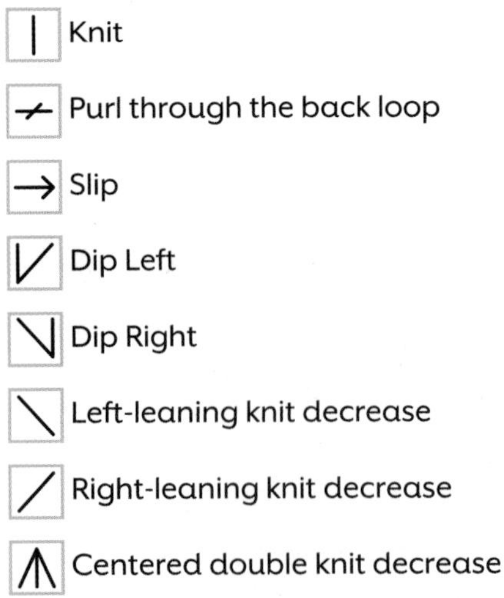

Sidereal

Yarn: Made with 275 yards of Skinny Singles, a fingering-weight yarn by Hedgehog Fibres, in the color Ghost. You may need up to 400 yards if you make a larger size or use a thinner yarn.

Size: Made in the 126-stitch size at a gauge of 7 stitches per inch. Use the chart to pick your gauge and size.

Notes: See the beginning of the book for more on how to pick a size, read a chart, make dip stitches, and decide how tall to make your hat.

	5.5 SPI	6 SPI	6.5 SPI	7 SPI
108 STS	21.5	19.75	18.25	17
114 STS	22.75	21	19.25	18
120 STS	24	22	20.25	18.75
126 STS	25.25	23	21.25	19.75
132 STS	26.5	24.25	22.25	20.75
138 STS	27.5	25.25	23.25	21.75

Cast on: Cast on 108 [114, 120, 126, 132, 138] stitches. Place marker. Join for working in the round.

Brim: Work the Rib Chart until brim reaches desired height. Shown here at 6 inches.

Body: Work the Main Chart until hat reaches desired height before decreases. Stop after completing row 9 of the Main Chart. Shown here at 5 inches.

Decreases: Before you start the decreases, shift the start of your round back 2 stitches. To do this, remove the start of round marker. Undo the 2 stitches you just worked. Replace your start of round marker. You've moved the start of the round 2 stitches to the right.

Work the Decrease Chart once. 18 [19, 20, 21, 22, 23] stitches remain. Work 9 [9, 10, 10, 11, 11] left-leaning twisted knit decreases and knit 0 [1, 0, 1, 0, 1] through the back loop. 9 [10, 10, 11, 11, 12] stitches remain.

Finishing: Remove marker, draw the yarn through remaining stitches. Weave in ends. Block.

Rib Chart

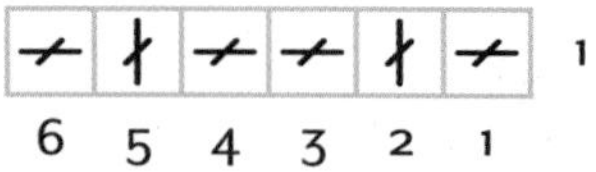

Main Chart

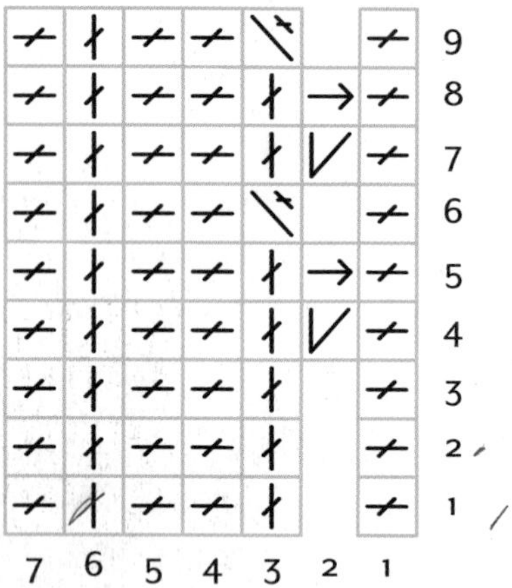

Dip Left: Yarn behind, count left 4 stitches and down to the untwisted stitch from row 1 (that's 3 rows for the Dip Left on row 4, 6 rows for the Dip Left on row 7). Pull a loop through.

Left-leaning twisted knit decrease: Insert the right needle from the right to the left into the back loops of 2 stitches. Knit both together.

Left-leaning half-twisted knit decrease: Slip 1 knitwise. Return slipped stitch to the left needle. Insert the right needle from the right to the left into 2 stitches. Knit both together.

This is *just* like a regular left-leaning knit decrease (sometimes called an ssk), except you're slipping 1 stitch, not 2. That keeps the uppermost stitch (the long loop you created a few rows before) untwisted and keeps the lowermost stitch twisted as it has been all along.

Slip: Slip 1 as if to purl with yarn in back.

Knit

Knit through the back loop

Purl through the back loop

Slip

Dip Left

Left-leaning half-twisted knit decrease

Decrease Chart

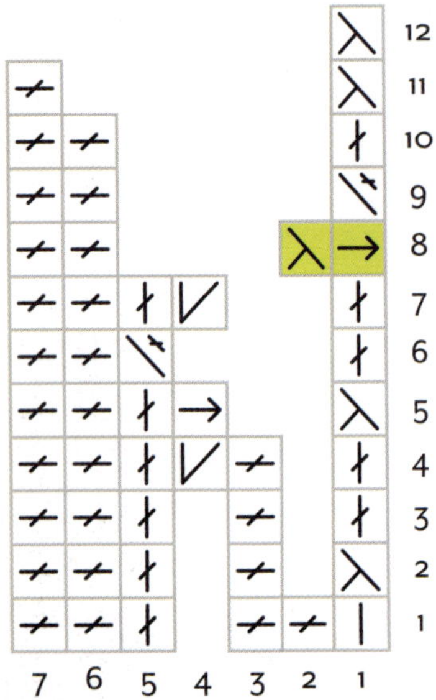

Knit

Knit through the back loop

Purl through the back loop

Slip

Dip Left

Left-leaning half-twisted knit decrease

Left-leaning twisted knit decrease

See special instructions in the notes at right

Note: Before you start the Decrease Chart, be sure you've **moved the start of your round** back 2 stitches (described in more detail in the decreases section above).

The **decreases on row 8 of the Decrease Chart** require extra attention. On row 8, you want to work a decrease using the stitches in column 1 and column 5. But the elongated stitch you made on row 7 is between these stitches so it is in the way.

To handle this, slip 1 stitch to your right needle. Slip the elongated stitch off your left needle and let it hang free in front of your work. Return the slipped stitch on your right to your left needle. Grab the elongated stitch and put it on your right needle (being careful to maintain its orientation). Work a left-leaning twisted knit decrease with the first 2 stitches on your left needle.

Ecliptic

Yarn: Made with 225 yards of Silk Blend, a DK-weight yarn by Manos Del Uruguay, in the color Ice Melt. You may need up to 400 yards if you make a larger size or use a thinner yarn.

Size: Made in the 108-stitch size at a gauge of 5.5 stitches per inch. Use the chart to pick your gauge and size.

Notes: See the beginning of the book for more on how to pick a size, read a chart, make dip stitches, and decide how tall to make your hat.

	5.5 SPI	6 SPI	6.5 SPI	7 SPI
108 STS	21.5	19.75	18.25	17
114 STS	22.75	21	19.25	18
120 STS	24	22	20.25	18.75
126 STS	25.25	23	21.25	19.75
132 STS	26.5	24.25	22.25	20.75
138 STS	27.5	25.25	23.25	21.75

Cast on: Cast on 108 [114, 120, 126, 132, 138] stitches. Place marker. Join for working in the round.

Brim: Work the Rib Chart until brim reaches desired height. Shown here at 5.5 inches.

Body: Work the Main Chart until hat reaches desired height before decreases. Stop after completing row 9 of the Main Chart. Shown here at 5 inches.

Decreases: Work the Decrease Chart once. 18 [19, 20, 21, 22, 23] stitches remain. Work 9 [9, 10, 10, 11, 11] left-leaning knit decreases and knit 0 [1, 0, 1, 0, 1]. 9 [10, 10, 11, 11, 12] stitches remain.

Finishing: Remove marker, draw the yarn through remaining stitches. Weave in ends. Block.

Rib Chart

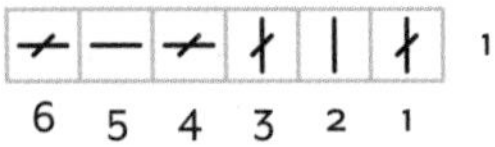

Main Chart

Decrease Chart

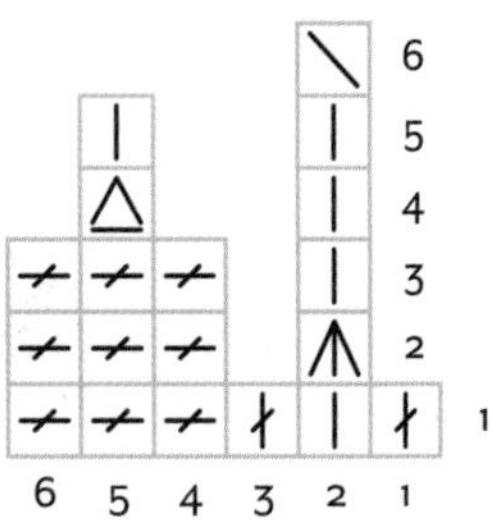

Dip Down: Yarn behind, count left 1 stitch and down 7 rows. Pull a loop through. Slip the next stitch on your left needle off and let it unravel down until it's caught by your elongated loop of yarn.

Left-leaning knit decrease: Slip 1 knitwise. Slip another 1 knitwise. Return slipped stitches to the left needle. Insert the right needle from the right to the left into the back loops of both stitches. Knit both together.

Centered double knit decrease: Slip 2 together at the same time as if to knit 2 together. Knit 1. Pass the slipped stitches over.

Centered twisted double purl decrease: Slip 1 as if to purl. Slip 1 as if to knit. Return the 2 slipped stitches to the left needle. Slip 2 together at the same time as if to purl 2 together through the back loop (swing your right needle tip around behind your fabric and come into those 2 stitches from the left). Purl 1. Pass the slipped stitches over.

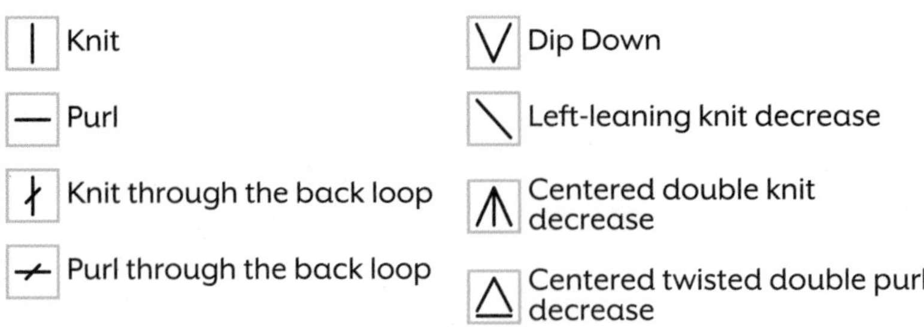

Ephemeris

Yarn: Made with 300 yards of Satchel, a fingering-weight yarn by Mrs. Crosby, in the color Greystone. You may need up to 400 yards if you make a larger size or use a thinner yarn.

Size: Made in the 128-stitch size at a gauge of 6.5 stitches per inch. Use the chart to pick your gauge and size.

Notes: See the beginning of the book for more on how to pick a size, read a chart, make dip stitches, and decide how tall to make your hat.

	5.5 SPI	6 SPI	6.5 SPI	7 SPI
104 STS	20.75	19	17.5	16.25
112 STS	22.5	20.5	19	17.5
120 STS	24	22	20.25	18.75
128 STS	25.5	23.5	21.75	20
136 STS	27.25	25	23	21.25

Cast on: Cast on 104 [112, 120, 128, 136] stitches. Place marker. Join for working in the round.

Brim: Work the Rib Chart until brim reaches desired height. Shown here at 5 inches.

Body: Work the Main Chart until hat reaches desired height before decreases. Stop after completing row 6 or 12 of the Main Chart. Shown here at 6.5 inches.

Decreases: If you stopped after completing row 12 of the Main Chart, shift the start of your round back 2 stitches (if you stopped after row 6, you don't need to do anything). To do this, remove the start of round marker. Undo the 2 stitches you just worked. Replace your start of round marker. You've moved the start of the round 2 stitches to the right.

Work the Decrease Chart once. 13 [14, 15, 16, 17] stitches remain.

Finishing: Remove marker, draw the yarn through remaining stitches. Weave in ends. Block.

Rib Chart

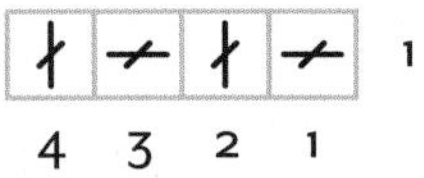

Main Chart

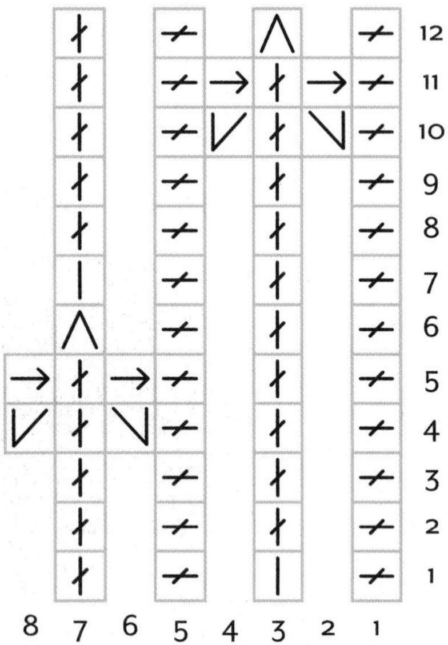

Note: When you work the very last Dip Left of the round on row 4, you'll count down one extra row. When you work the very first Dip Right of the round on row 10, you'll count down one fewer row. But in both cases it will be easy, because you'll be going into the untwisted stitch from row 1 or 7, so you'll know just where to aim.

Dip Left: Yarn behind, count left 2 stitches and down 3 rows. Pull a loop through.

Dip Right: Yarn behind, count right 2 stitches and down 4 rows. Pull a loop through.

Centered twisted double knit decrease: Slip 1 as if to purl. Remount the next stitch so it is rotated 180 degrees (one half turn) clockwise. Return the slipped stitch to the left needle. Slip 2 together at the same time as if to knit 2 together. Knit 1. Pass the slipped stitches over.

Left-leaning twisted knit decrease: Insert the right needle from the right to the left into the back loops of 2 stitches. Knit both together.

Slip: Slip 1 as if to purl with yarn in back.

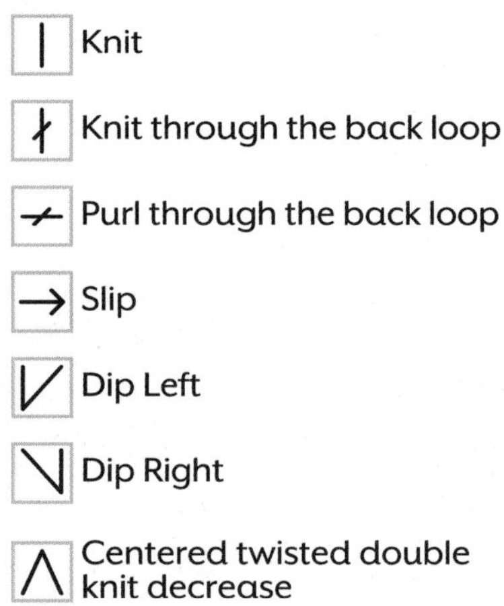

Decrease Chart

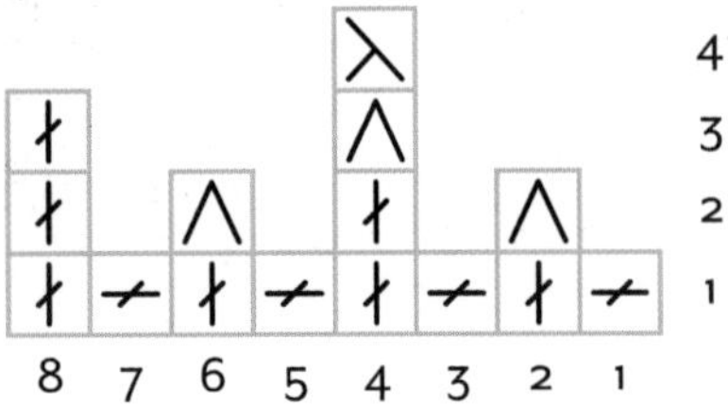

Note: If you stopped after completing round 12, before you start the Decrease Chart, be sure you've **MOVED THE START OF YOUR ROUND** back 2 stitches (described in more detail in the decreases section above).

- Knit through the back loop
- Purl through the back loop
- Centered twisted double knit decrease
- Left-leaning twisted knit decrease

Cowls

Having too much fun to stop? Want to make a companion piece to go with your hat? How about a cowl!

All of these stitches look lovely on both sides, so they make fabulous cowls. And it's very easy to turn a hat pattern into a cowl pattern. We just need to talk a bit about sizing.

The charts to the right show you the size of your cowl at various gauges and stitch counts. The smallest sizes will fit close around your neck. The largest ones will either hang down quite far or loop around twice.

Cast on: Cast on 144 [160, 176, 192, 208, 224, 240] (for Constellate or Ephemeris) or 156 [168, 180, 192, 204, 216, 228, 240] (for Sidereal or Ecliptic). Place marker. Join for working in the round.

Rib: Work the appropriate Rib Chart for 1 inch.

Body: Work the appropriate Main Chart until cowl is 1 inch shorter than desired height (stop after completing the last row of the appropriate Main Chart).

Rib: Work the appropriate Rib Chart for 1 inch.

Finishing: Bind off. Weave in ends. Block.

Constellate or Ephemeris

	5.5 SPI	6 SPI	6.5 SPI	7 SPI
144 STS	26.25	24	22.25	20.5
160 STS	29	26.75	24.5	22.75
176 STS	32	29.25	27	25.25
192 STS	35	32.25	29.75	27.5
208 STS	37.75	34.75	32	29.75
224 STS	40.75	37.25	34.5	32
240 STS	43.75	40	37	34.25

Sidereal or Ecliptic

	5.5 SPI	6 SPI	6.5 SPI	7 SPI
156 STS	28.25	26	24	22.25
168 STS	30.5	28	25.75	24
180 STS	32.75	30	27.75	25.75
192 STS	35	32	29.5	27.5
204 STS	37	34	31.5	29.25
216 STS	39.25	36	33.25	30.75
228 STS	41.5	38	35	32.5
240 STS	43.75	40	37	34.25

Dip Stitch Variants

Dip stitches lend themselves to endless variations. I've provided four of my favorites here (and shown both the right and wrong sides of several of them). But I know there are many other possibilities, and I encourage you to experiment and find something you love!

While you play with these variations, keep a few things in mind. First, these charts are all for working **IN THE ROUND**. It's possible to work these stitches flat, but it's somewhere between fiddly and tricky, and I don't recommend it.

Second, remember that the **BLANK WHITE SQUARES** are just placeholders to keep the charts lined up. You don't make a stitch for them, just skip over them and move on to the next square with a symbol in it.

Finally, you'll notice **HEAVY LINES** on some of the charts. Don't worry, they're nothing scary.

Heavy horizontal lines separate any setup rows from the main body of the chart. Work the setup rows (the ones below the heavy horizontal line) only once. Repeat the main stitch pattern (the rows above the heavy horizontal line) as needed.

Vertical lines are a little trickier. If you're working the stitch in a continuous field over the entire surface of your fabric (like in the hats in the book), you'll just work the main stitch repeat (the columns to the right of the heavy vertical line) and ignore any columns to the left of the vertical line. But if you want to work the stitch as a panel (say down the back of a glove or the front of a sweater), you'll probably want the pattern to be symmetric. To do that, work the main stitch repeat as many times as you want, then work the columns to the left of the heavy vertical line once.

Constellate Variant

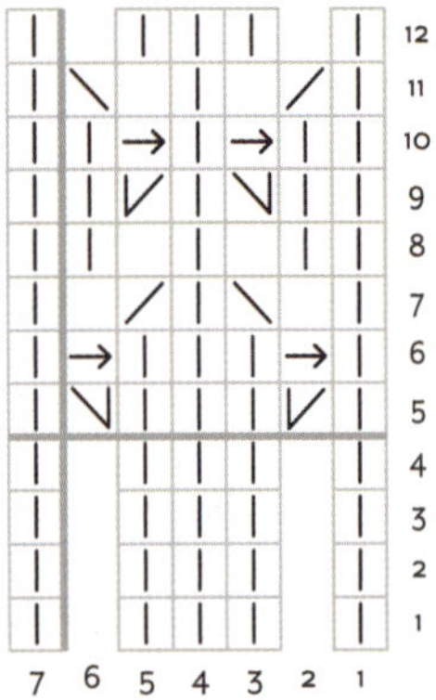

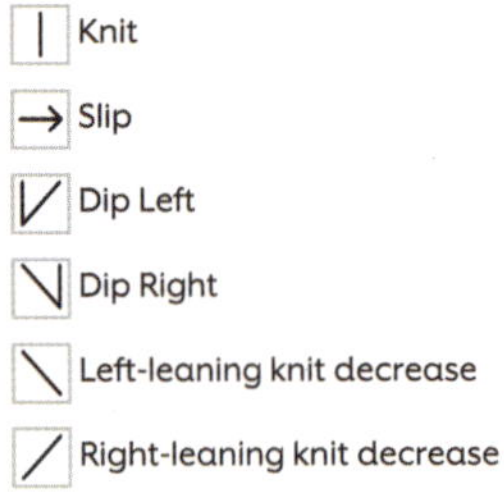

Note: See the section on Dip Stitch Variants for information about the heavy lines on the chart.

Dip Left: Yarn behind, count left 2 stitches and down 4 rows. Pull a loop through.

Dip Right: Yarn behind, count right 2 stitches and down 5 rows. Pull a loop through.

Left-leaning knit decrease: Slip 1 knitwise. Slip another 1 knitwise. Return slipped stitches to the left needle. Insert the right needle from the right to the left into the back loops of both stitches. Knit both together.

Right-leaning knit decrease: Knit 2 together.

Slip: Slip 1 as if to purl with yarn in back.

Sidereal Variant

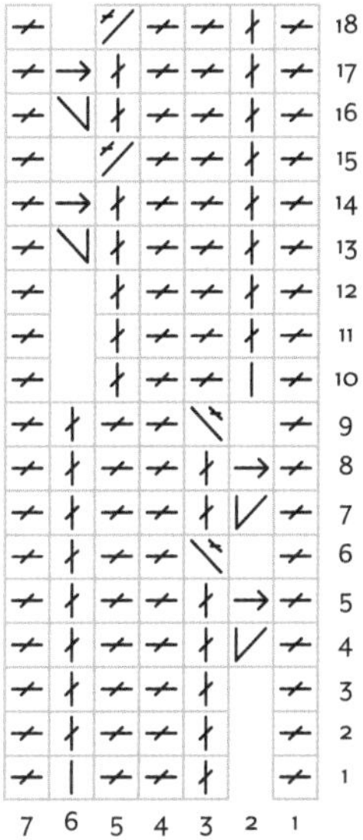

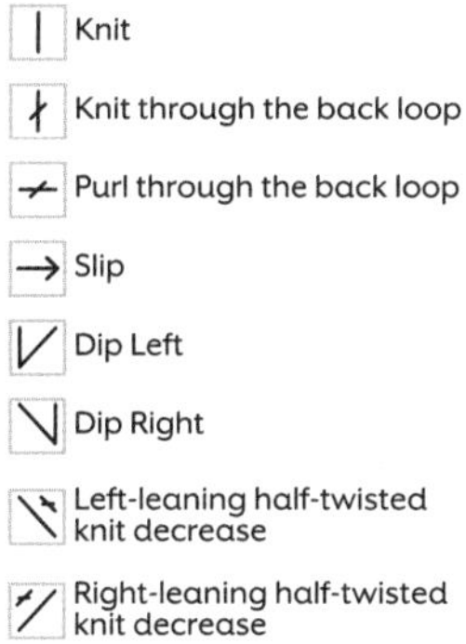

Dip Left: Yarn behind, count left 4 stitches and down to the untwisted stitch from row 1 (that's 3 rows for the Dip Left on row 4, 6 rows for the Dip Left on row 7). Pull a loop through.

Dip Right: Yarn behind, count right 4 stitches and down to the untwisted stitch from row 10 (that's 4 rows for the Dip Right on row 13, 7 rows for the Dip Right on row 16). Pull a loop through.

Left-leaning half-twisted knit decrease: Slip 1 knitwise. Return slipped stitch to the left needle. Insert the right needle from the right to the left into 2 stitches. Knit both together.

Right-leaning half-twisted knit decrease: Remount the next stitch so it is rotated 180 degrees (one half turn) clockwise. Knit 2 together.

Slip: Slip 1 as if to purl with yarn in back.

Ecliptic Variant

- Knit
- Purl
- Knit through the back loop
- Purl through the back loop
- Dip Down

Note: See the section on Dip Stitch Variants for information about the heavy lines on the chart.

Dip Down: Yarn behind, count left 1 stitch and down 6 rows. Pull a loop through. Slip the next stitch off your left needle and let it unravel down until it's caught by your elongated loop of yarn.

Ephemeris Variant

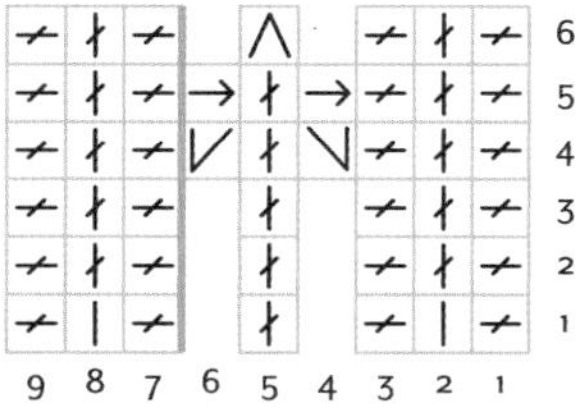

- Knit
- Knit through the back loop
- Purl through the back loop
- Slip
- Dip Left
- Dip Right
- Centered twisted double knit decrease

Note: See the section on Dip Stitch Variants for information about the heavy line on the chart.

Dip Left: Yarn behind, count left 2 stitches and down 3 rows. Pull a loop through.

Dip Right: Yarn behind, count right 2 stitches and down 4 rows. Pull a loop through.

Slip: Slip 1 as if to purl with yarn in back.

Centered twisted double knit decrease: Slip 1 as if to purl. Remount the next stitch so it is rotated 180 degrees (one half turn) clockwise. Return the slipped stitch to the left needle. Slip 2 together at the same time as if to knit 2 together. Knit 1. Pass the slipped stitches over.

Sources

These hats are given in lots of gauges so they will work beautifully with fingering, sport, DK, or light worsted-weight yarns. Just be aware that dip stitches take a bit of extra yarn (all those long loops are yarn fiends), so you will likely need more yarn than you usually do for a hat or cowl. It's probably a good idea to have an extra skein on hand.

Constellate: Tosh Merino Light by Madelinetosh in Calligraphy.
MADELINETOSH.COM

Sidereal: Skinny Singles by Hedgehog Fibres in Ghost.
HEDGEHOGFIBRES.COM

Ecliptic: Silk Blend by Manos Del Uruguay in Ice Melt.
MANOSYARNS.COM

Ephemeris: Satchel by Mrs. Crosby in Greystone.
MRSCROSBYPLAYS.COM

Charts: Made with Stitchmastery.
STITCHMASTERY.COM

Illustrations: By Lana Holden.

Thanks

First and foremost, I want to thank everyone who saw these stitches and loved them as much as I did. Without your enthusiastic support, I'd never have decided to share this odd little obsession of mine with the world. So, to everyone who watched these grow on Instagram and Ravelry and my website (and said kind things about them), thank you. There wouldn't be a book without you!

Then there are the folks who helped move the book from an idea to something you can hold in your hands. Lana Holden served as editor and illustrator extraordinaire (and provided me with more than my fair share of pep talks along the way). Thank her when your knitting goes smoothly and it sounds like I know what I'm talking about. Heather Ordover made sure I actually said what I meant (and kept me entertained with CraftLit, her delightful podcast, through many hours of knitting). Brian Glenn listened to no end of stream-of-consciousness rambles about the book as it took shape, played photographer's assistant as I tromped through the woods and the rocks in search of just the right shot, read this whole thing many more times than anyone should, and generally kept me sane (and fed) as the book came together. Thank him when I am brave enough to tackle the next book!

Other Works

Looking for more? Well I'm flattered!

I've been doing this for a while now, and the books do seem to stack up. These are a few of my most recent projects (and I suspect there will be even more in the very near future).

If you want more information about them (or my individual patterns, or whatever else I'm up to at the moment), you can always find it at **PANTSVILLEPRESS.COM**.

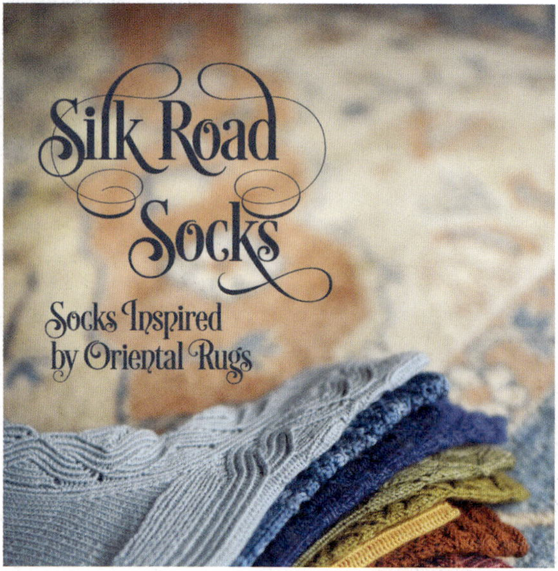